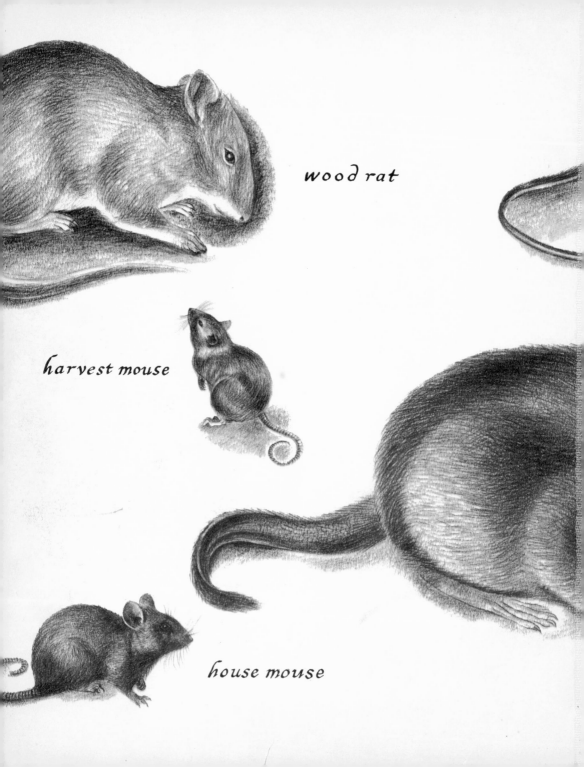

wood rat

harvest mouse

house mouse

white footed mouse

kangaroo rat

golden hamsters

muskrat

GOLDEN HAMSTERS

by **HERBERT S. ZIM**

illustrated by **herschel wartik**

WILLIAM MORROW & COMPANY, New York, 1951

Thanks are due to Dr. Frank G. Ashbrook,

U. S. Fish and Wildlife Service,

and to

Dr. Orson N. Eaton

U. S. Department of Agriculture,

for reading and criticizing the manuscript.

. . . . . .

No other animals ever became popular as fast as the golden hamsters. Twenty years ago they were unknown. Today thousands of people have hamsters for pets. They are used in schools and are important in science laboratories.

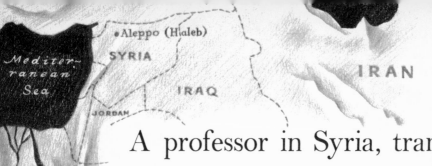

A professor in Syria, tramping the dusty fields near Aleppo one April morning in 1930, never dreamed of this while he studied and collected native animals. He stopped at the burrow of a common hamster, very much like dozens of others he had seen. Professor Aronin decided to ex-

plore this one, and so he began to dig. Finally, at the end of an eight-foot tunnel, he found a mother with twelve young in her nest. He put them in a cage to take back to the Hebrew University in Jerusalem with him. Hamsters had never been kept in captivity before.

Some of the young died on the way; some died later, till only one male and two females remained. But these ate well, grew fast, and became tame. After four months one female had a new litter—the first hamsters to be born in captivity. As these grew up, the scientists at the university watched and

studied them. Would they make
a new laboratory animal?

Laboratory animals are those
used by scientists in experiments
to learn about foods, drugs,
and diseases. Many thousands of
experiments with rats, mice,
dogs, guinea pigs, and monkeys
have provided doctors with in-
formation which has helped to
save countless human lives.
But all animals do not react in
the same way toward drugs and
germs. So scientists are always
on the lookout for new and

more useful laboratory animals.

Two pairs of hamsters were sent to a laboratory in England where they were used with great success. Other hamsters went to doctors in France. In 1938, hamsters were shipped to this country for the first time, to scientists of the United States Public Health Service at Carville,

Louisiana. All the hamsters that have found their way to Europe and America were offspring of that one litter collected in Syria in 1930. All the hamsters in schools, museums, pet stores, laboratories, and homes today came from those few animals too.

These little animals, which became so numerous and popular in the short space of twenty years, are soft, attractive creatures with golden-brown fur, large black eyes, short legs, and even shorter tails. They are often very tame, and people who have raised them think they have no equal as pets. Whether they are called Syrian hamsters, golden hamsters, or golden "bears," all tame hamsters are just the same. The Syrian or golden hamster is closely related to all the other

European hamsters

wild hamsters in Europe and Asia.

The family of rodents or gnawing mammals, to which hamsters belong, includes over a thousand small animals living all over the world. In this country,

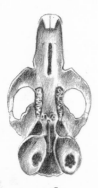

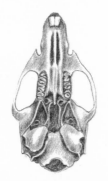

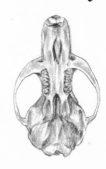

vole   *cotton rat*   *hamster*

the close relatives of hamsters include meadow mice, pack rats, and muskrats. The lemmings of the north are relatives of hamsters too. Squirrels, chipmunks, and prairie dogs are less closely related to hamsters.

hamster   Norwegian lemming

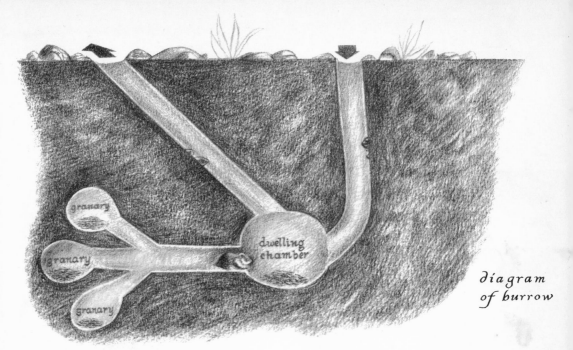

granary

granary

granary

dwelling chamber

diagram of burrow

The hamsters of the Old World are animals of fields, meadows, and open places. They live in rock piles and fence rows, burrowing down in tunnels two to ten feet long. There the female builds a nest and raises her young. The hamsters store,

inside their burrows, food which
they have gathered from nearby
fields. This habit has given
hamsters their name, from the
German word *hamstern,* meaning
to hoard or store.

cheek pouches full   *cheek pouches empty*

     Hamsters stuff the food they have gathered into a pair of cheek pouches. When the pouches are full of grain, they bulge like a bad case of mumps. Then the hamster hurries back to its burrow where, with a quick movement of its front paws, it empties the grain into a storage pile. Sixty to a hundred pounds of grain have been found in the burrows of some of the European hamsters. It is no wonder that wild hamsters are heartily disliked by farmers.

Hamsters sometimes rob the nests of ground birds and eat their eggs or young. Now and then they eat lizards, insects, or worms. In turn, they have enemies which eat them—snakes, hawks, owls, weasels, and foxes. In their native lands these enemies help keep hamsters in check, yet they still manage to rob the farmer.

hamster enemies

marten

fox

hawk

owl

snake

man

Full-grown golden hamsters are only four to five inches long and weigh only four to five ounces, so they need less room than any other small mammals except white mice. Hamsters grow fast, breed rapidly, and remain healthy when they are caged. They are attractive, clean, easy to house, simple to feed, and interesting to watch as they grow and raise their families.

This has made them popular as pets. The rapidity with which hamsters grow and breed is most unusual. No other animals living in captivity grow up as rapidly as hamsters. No others can raise as many young in as short a time.

Hamsters should be kept in simple metal cages, for they can gnaw their way out of wood. A wood framework covered with

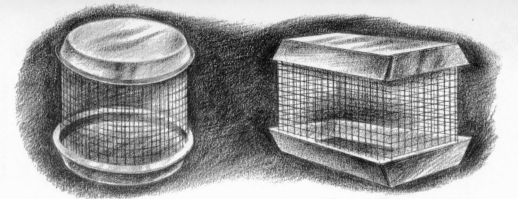

quarter-inch or half-inch wire mesh (hardware cloth) may be used, but an all-metal cage is easier to clean. The simplest cage can be made from two deep baking tins, round or square, with a cylinder or square of hardware cloth ten inches high, set between.

Allow enough wire mesh to fit the pans snugly, and fasten the ends together with several

all you need is:

a wire cutter

hardware cloth
to fit pan

allow plenty overlap

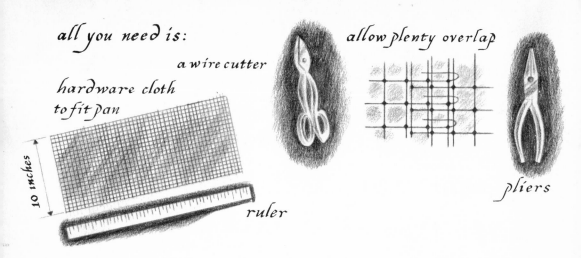

10 inches

ruler

pliers

how to make a baking-tin cage

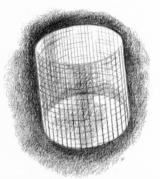

roll hardware cloth
into a cylinder

pie tins

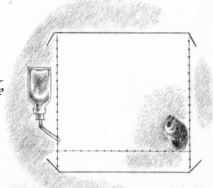

self-feed water bottle

self-cleaning tray

inches of overlap. Other designs with hardware cloth are possible. Make plans of your own, allowing about one square foot of floor space for each hamster. A female has ample room to raise her young in a cage 12 by 18 inches and 12 inches high.

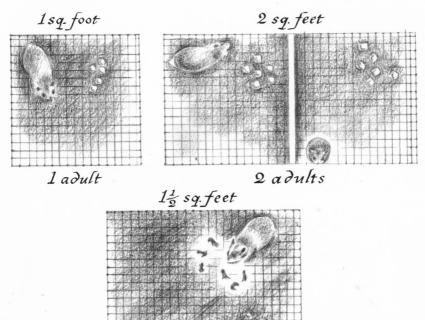

1 sq. foot

1 adult

2 sq. feet

2 adults

1½ sq. feet

mother and young

Begin with two single cages or with a large divided cage. Keep the male and female hamsters apart till you wish to breed them. Cages can be put in any convenient, light, airy place.

Hamsters do best when the temperature is between 50 and 80 degrees. If it is warmer, be sure the cages are well ventilated. When it is colder than 40 degrees, hamsters stop moving around and hibernate. They sleep till it becomes warmer

hamsters are active at 75°

hamsters are inactive at 40°

again. Cover the bottom of the baking-tin cage with an inch or two of coarse sawdust or wood shavings. Self-cleaning cages with hardware cloth bottoms do not need sawdust, but should have material inside for the hamster's nest. Shavings or excelsior (shredded wood) will do. A piece of hemp rope cut into six-inch lengths and unraveled makes excellent nesting material.

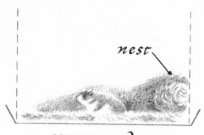

nest

coarse sawdust

self-cleaning cage

nest

sawdust or shredded paper

The hamster's habit of storing food makes a food container unnecessary. Wire a small jar of water to a side or corner of the cage so the hamster can't tip it over. Another way to supply

water is through a gravity watering bottle which, because of its curved spout, gives the hamster a fresh flow of water as long as it is drinking. The water does not run out while the bottle is standing, because the tube is narrow.

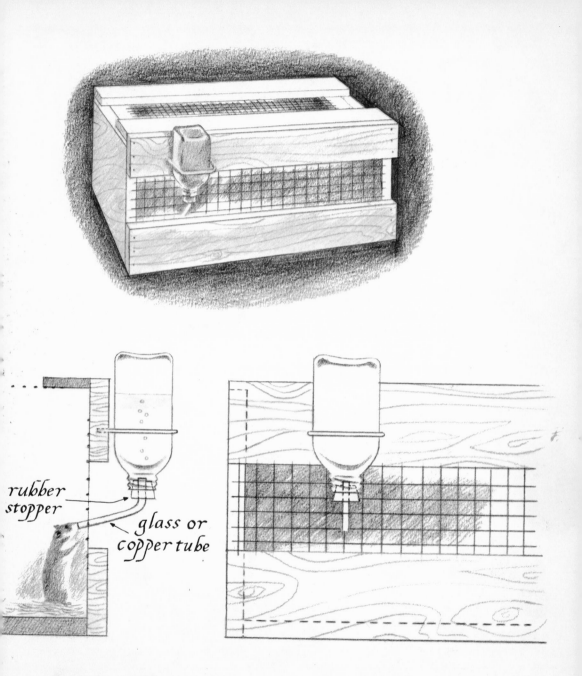

rubber
stopper

glass or
copper tube

gravity watering bottle

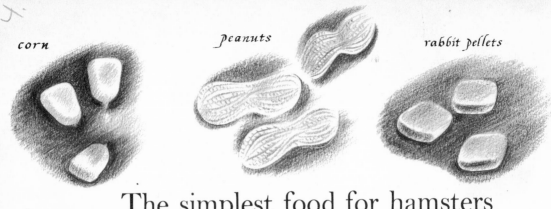

corn

peanuts

rabbit pellets

beans

grain

The simplest food for hamsters is ordinary dog biscuits, plus a small supply of green vegetables, bits of fresh fruit, and a scrap of meat now and then. Vegetables provide hamsters with water. If they have enough green food, hamsters do not drink. Vary the diet with nuts, corn, wheat,

peas

dog biscuit

cabbage

hard food – teeth sharp   soft food – teeth overgrown

peas, or beans, but do not feed
too much or too often. Always
be sure hamsters have rabbit
pellets, dog biscuits, or grain, as
they need hard food to keep
their teeth short and sharp.
About a tablespoonful of grain,
two pellets, or a dog biscuit
daily is enough for a hamster.

meat

bread crust

carrot   potato

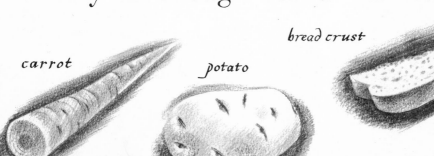

Anything extra will be stored. If it is more convenient, feed hamsters every other day. Since they are clean and free of odors, sawdust can be changed once a week.

To begin raising hamsters, start with a single pair, preferably a full-grown male and female. If you buy half-grown hamsters of uncertain age, keep them separate and do not attempt breeding for two or three weeks. During that time handle the hamsters and let them become used to you. This may require

patience when they come from large colonies and are not used to being handled. Frightened hamsters can and do bite. Their sharp front teeth may draw blood. Pick up a hamster by the loose skin at the back of its neck. Use your other hand to support

its body. Wear gloves at first. Your hamsters will soon be sitting quietly in the palm of your hand or will be crawling up and down your arm, sniffing and exploring. When you know how to handle hamsters, it is easy to tell the male from the female.

Lift and hold them so you can examine the undersides. Notice the difference in shape of the rear of the body. The testicles of the male, right at the base of its tail give its body a tapering shape. The female is

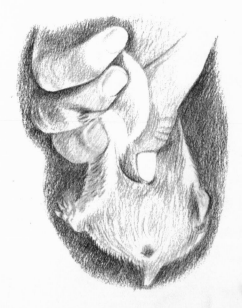

male   *female*

shorter and more rounded at
the back. With some practice
you can tell the sex of hamsters
as young as ten days old. The
nipples of the female appear as
two rows of dots about this time.

Breeding is likely to be the

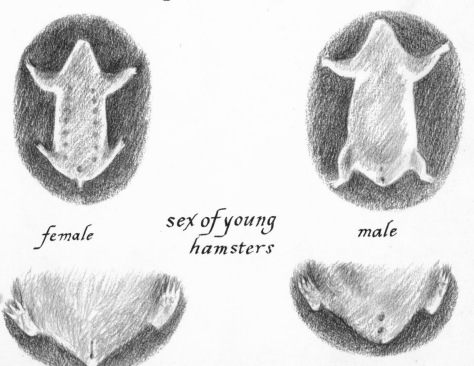

female   *sex of young*   male
hamsters

next step. Hamsters are old enough to breed at eight weeks and the female will continue to bear young for a year or so. By then hamsters are past their prime and, though they may live for two years or more, it is not good practice to breed old animals.

Once the male hamster is mature, it is ready to mate at

any time. The female hamster is ready to mate every four days. Hamsters usually mate in the evenings. Place the female in the cage of the male toward evening. Mating should follow soon, and the female should be removed after an hour or so. If the pair fight and continue fighting, remove the female until another time.

Pedigree – Hamster no. 38. sex male			breeding record
		9	Nov. 23 '51 to no. 46
26		grandfather	Dec 14 '51 to no 53
father	6		
	3	grandmother	
18		grandfather	
mother	7		
		grandmother	
Sept. 22 1951	9		
date of birth		no. in litter	

september

sun	mon	tue	wed	thu	fri	sat
		mated				1
2	3	(4)	5	6	7	8
9	10	11	12	13	14	15
16	17	18	19	(20) *young* 21 *due*		22
23/30	24	25	26	27	28	29

Make a record of the date
when mating takes place. The
young will be born sixteen days
later, perhaps less by three or
four hours. Mark the date on a
calendar and check. If your
female is very tame, try to keep
a record of her weight from
the time she has mated till just
before her young are born.

Her weight may nearly double as the five to thirteen young develop inside her body. An average litter is six to eight.

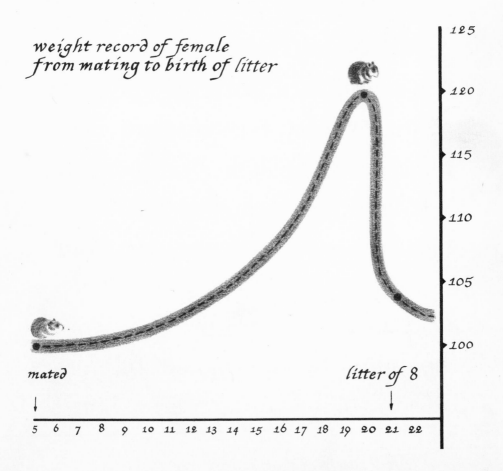

weight record of female
from mating to birth of litter

mated

litter of 8

5 6 7 8 9 10 11 12 13 14 15 16 17 18 19 20 21 22

Between the time of mating and the time the young are born, the female does not require special care. Give her a small dish of milk besides her regular food. Keep this up after the young are born till they are able to care for themselves. The female will build her nest or will rebuild one she already has. Give her scraps of cloth or tissue

paper to line her nest and make it softer and warmer. Do not handle or disturb the mother after the young are born, especially if it is her first litter. A frightened mother may kill her young and, for some reason, may eat them. Leave the mother alone for the first three or four days, if she has enough food and milk.

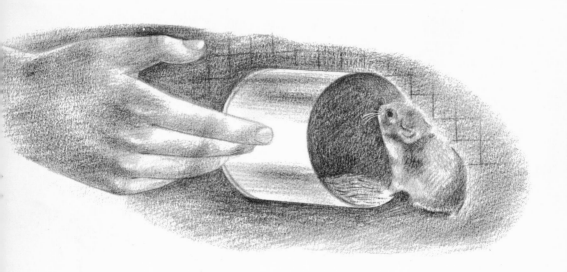

Even very tame hamsters act wilder just before and just after the young are born and are more likely to bite then. To clean the cage, coax the mother out by placing food in a tin can.

Set it on its side on the bottom of the cage. As the mother enters to see what is there, lift the can with her inside. Some mothers remain tame and do not mind being handled.

The blind, naked baby hamsters are very tiny. A litter of eight to twelve weighs less than one ounce. But they grow rapidly. In three days the skin

begins to darken and hair begins to appear. Eight-day-old babies begin to nibble on solid food. At two weeks their eyes open and by that time they can be handled as pets. Soon the mother stops nursing the young, and when they are three or four weeks old, each baby hamster weighs about an ounce and is

two weeks old

on its own. The young should then be separated from the mother, who is ready to raise another family a month after the last litter was born. At five

four weeks old

or six weeks, young hamsters
are old enough to breed, so
males and females should be
separated before then.

The fact that hamsters breed so rapidly and have so many young creates problems. Be sure you have enough space, food, extra cages, and time to care for the hamsters before you breed too many. Officials of the

United States Fish and Wildlife
Service and the Department of
Agriculture are worried about
these problems also. As more
and more people raise hamsters,
they fear what might happen
if someone had too many
hamsters and wanted to get rid
of them.

cotton rat

prairie dog

wood rat

gopher

native rodent pests

meadow mouse

ground squirrel

These experts know that wild hamsters could cause farmers as much trouble as field mice, gophers, or prairie dogs. They could live and breed in all but the most northern parts of our country. Perhaps hawks, owls,

average temperature above freezing in winter

area in which hamsters might thrive if they became established

and foxes would destroy hamsters that escaped. But the experts remember what happened to other animals which people turned loose or which escaped by accident.

starling

english sparrow

house mouse

norway rat

pests introduced into
the United States

tent caterpillar

gypsy moth

Just a century ago English
sparrows were freed in Brooklyn
in the hope that they would
destroy harmful insects. Instead,
English sparrows have become

pests which have made life harder for our native birds. Starlings are another foreign bird we should never have turned loose here. The Norway rat and the common house mouse escaped from European ships back in colonial days. We are

still trying to get rid of them. An Englishman in Australia freed some rabbits in the hope of having good hunting. Since then, that country has spent millions of dollars on fencing, poisons, and hunts to keep rabbits under control.

These mistakes with animals explain why scientists are afraid of the results if hamsters got loose and ran wild in this country. They know how fast hamsters can breed. A single female may give birth to from

fifty to a hundred young in a
year, and before the year is
out many of these young will
be having litters of their own.
If they were wild, most of them
would feed on grain and other
farm crops.

in half a year two hamsters might increase to two hundred or more

		male	female			total young
weeks	0	🐹	🐹			= 2
	2	🐹	🐹 + 🐹🐹🐹🐹 🐹🐹🐹🐹 8 young			= 10
	4					
	6					
	8	🐹	🐹 + 🐹🐹🐹🐹 🐹🐹🐹🐹 8 nearly grown	+ 🐹🐹🐹🐹 8 young		= 18
	10					
	12					
	14	🐹	🐹 + 56 young and their offspring			= 58
	16					
	18					
	20	🐹	🐹 + 96 young and their offspring			= 98
	22					
	24	🐹	🐹 + 168 young and their offspring			= 170

This means that everyone who enjoys the fun of keeping and raising hamsters must take a responsibility that people who raise goldfish or canaries do not share. If you raise hamsters for fun or for study, be sure they do not escape to establish wild colonies. Guard against this one danger that might turn a handsome and interesting pet into a dangerous and expensive pest.